Firefly

poems by

Ellen Austin-Li

Finishing Line Press
Georgetown, Kentucky

Firefly

*For Sharon, who showed me the way
and would have wanted me to help
those who still suffer*

Copyright © 2019 by Ellen Austin-Li
ISBN 978-1-63534-913-9 First Edition
All rights reserved under International and Pan-American Copyright Conventions. No part of this book may be reproduced in any manner whatsoever without written permission from the publisher, except in the case of brief quotations embodied in critical articles and reviews.

ACKNOWLEDGMENTS

The following poems appeared in previous publications, some in earlier versions, thanks to the generosity of several poetry editors:

"Firefly" in *Artemis*, May, 2018.
"Cocoon" and "Two Ships" in LA Writers Tribe Review.
"Thirteen Ways of Looking at Cowboy Boots" on *The Poet's Craft*, the webpage of Pauletta Hansel, Poet Laureate of Cincinnati, 2016-2018.
"House of Trees" on Pauletta Hansel's webpage, *The Poet's Craft*, September 25, 2017.
"Cameo Moon" on the Public Library of Cincinnati and Hamilton County's website, a winner of 2016's "Through the Garden" poetry contest, co-sponsored by the Greater Cincinnati Writers League.
"Wild Hive" in *Pine Mountain Sand and Gravel*, Fall 2018.
"Awakening" and "Sliver of Power" in *Amethyst Review* in Oct. & Nov. 2018.
"Thawing with Frost" and "Amends to My Father" in Green Briar Review, April 2019.

Publisher: Leah Maines
Editor: Christen Kincaid
Front Cover Design and Illustration: Elaine Olund
Author Photos: Suzann Fleming-Smith (inside)
　　　　　　　Ellen Austin-Li (back)

Printed in the USA on acid-free paper.
Order online: www.finishinglinepress.com
　　　　　　　also available on amazon.com

Author inquiries and mail orders:
Finishing Line Press
P. O. Box 1626
Georgetown, Kentucky 40324
U. S. A.

Table of Contents

Wild Hive 1
Caterpillar 2
What You Never Wanted (a Paradelle) 3
The Valiant 4
Scar 6
Firefly 7
Spin 8
Wild Women 9
Cocoon 10
The Failure of Geographic Cures 11
Otherworld 13
Awakening 14
For the Irish Girl Who Got Sober (Again) on St. Paddy's Day
   on a Cruise Ship 15
Two Ships 17
Dispirited 18
Amends to My Father, 1941 19
Ghost Bartender 21
The Cocktail Party 22
Thawing with Frost 23
Thirteen Ways of Looking at Cowboy Boots 25
House of Trees 28
Hymn 29
Sliver of Power 30
Cameo Moon 31
Resurrection 32

"You see, 'alcohol' in Latin is 'spiritus' and you use the same word for the highest religious experience as well as for the most depraving poison. The helpful formula therefore is: spiritus contra spiritum." (spirit against spirit)

—Carl Jung

Wild Hive

A rumble summoned my husband last spring
to rescue a beehive; he found it
hung like a tongue abuzz with hunger,
urgent hooligans hunkering around
a honeyed crux. He clipped the bunched
cluster, curried the tree branch, and dumped
it into a hovel.

He had three hives at the beginning
of winter, but only the mined line
survived this time. He thinks

       there's something in being wild
       that keeps things alive.

Caterpillar

An accounting of amorphous memory must
begin bursting pink with Bazooka Joe bubble gum, sticky hands plunged
into a Crackerjacks box, rummaging for a prize in miniature,
digging in plundered caramel-coated treasure
eager for an unlikely emerald. Back then,
the fervor of each moment was an adventure; now these memories are
ghosts, gleeful shadows of yesterday. My mother used to say, *Keep the
home fires burning*—words that stir nostalgia soup
for the Innocent days of childhood—followed by, *Be back in a
jiffy*, a cliché tossed over her shoulder as she drifted out of the
kitchen. Those days, the worst slight imaginable was being called *liar,
liar, pants on fire*; all was right with the world biking along the Erie Canal
munching a crisp, juicy-tart MacIntosh with one hand,
navigating the pebbly trail with the other,
or with an open paperback
perched in the apple tree,
queen of the jungle, legs swinging—until
rainstorms forced feet onto solid
soil. All this was before my metamorphosis, from timid caterpillar
to a full-fledged lunatic moth, drawn to the hottest flame—
underneath the sweet candy shell,
a veritable molten mass of a mess—what my mother always
warned against—
exactly what she said happens when
youngsters like me don't obey their elders, or some other calculated
zing that fed my larval stage.

What You Never Wanted (a Paradelle)

I am nothing, I'm invisible. You sat cross-legged, tearing at grass.
I am nothing, I'm invisible. You sat cross-legged, tearing at grass.
A little girl hid beneath the weeping willow.
A little girl hid beneath the weeping willow.
I'm invisible.   Beneath a willow you sat cross-legged,
a little girl weeping, hidden, tearing at grass   *I am nothing.*

What do you dream? What do you want to be when you grow up?
What do you dream? What do you want to be when you grow up?
Remember, no one likes a drunk girl.   Never, your mother said.
Remember, no one likes a drunk girl.   Never, your mother said.
A girl growing up wanting, remember when your mother said
    no one likes?
You never dreamed of becoming a drunk.

From the first time you sipped it, alcohol torched your trembling.
From the first time you sipped it, alcohol torched your trembling.
Drink filled in the outlines of your body.
Drink filled in the outlines of your body.
The outline of your body trembled, nothing filled it—
sipping alcohol torched from the first time.

When you were invisible, wanting filled your body,
outlined a little girl weeping. You sat trembling,
crossed-legged beneath a willow.   *I am nothing*
Do you remember the times growing up, tearing at grass, hiding?
From the first sip, alcohol torched your   *no one likes*—
becoming a drunk was never your dream.

The Valiant

When she first arrived home,
she was a shiny earth-brown stalwart
trimmed in gunmetal chrome,
a Plymouth sedan born to her name.
She stoically bore all manner of assault—
overpacked with teenaged girls in a chorus of hysteria,
she tilted sideways, slanted nearly ninety degrees,
precarious in an ice cream shop parking lot.
She groaned, in danger of rolling over,
as pubescent bodies slid across
her vanilla upholstery in gravitational glee.
She stayed grounded.

She endured a mud-caked rear end
when carelessly backed into
an overgrown hillside, her license plate left
dangling by one turf-encrusted bolt.
She suffered a fool's journey, fueled
by weed and Almaden wine,
over dark, snaking wooded roads
in the (she knew) vain quest to find
The Yellow Brick Road in Chittenango.
She steered, obedient.

She suffered the wrenching loss
of her antenna in a local bar's lot,
an effort to jimmy open her locked door—
she wasn't sure if she was more indignant
about her missing body part
or those two privileged passengers
coaxing a schoolmate from poorer circumstances
to break-in (it wasn't her fault
the keys were left dangling in her teeth).
She bruised.

She met her demise,
crashed kamikaze-like
into a barn on the shoulder of some back
country road. She saw it coming, felt
all the swerves and unsteady handling,
could do nothing
to stop her slow spin
across the solid white line.
She expired with her face pushed-in
to crumpled chest, wheel pressed
hard, pinning that young woman
bloody. Her horn silenced,
she died
Valiant.

Scar

My bare belly
is an alabaster mold, pasty pale
from forty years of darkness.
A plush ribbon of pink, marked
with silver striations, runs a zipper
from xiphoid to pubis—evidence
of Dr. Zaman's explorations
with surgical scalpel. He left me
lighter that night, pulled-out pulverized
spleen and liver lobe, plunked
them into the OR's metal bowl.

I awoke with Frankenstein's torso,
abdominal muscles stapled shut, rubber
drain stitched to my flank, membranes
meshed together with sutures. To laugh,
to cough, to sneeze felt too tender then,
as if these simple acts of living were enough
to tear me apart. Now, I carry my scars
in secret, hide them from the burning
eye of the sun. At night, I strip
daytime coverings and see this emblem
from when pain rode through me
in waves, before time's softening.

Firefly

Last night a firefly was trapped
inside my bedroom, frantic
fluorescence, neon green
darting, looking for escape;
moments of illumination
were dashes across a black page.

I opened the screen door,
tried to show her the way
to freedom, how easy it would be
to regain her life,
but the firefly flew
deeper into a trap,
further inside
her dark prison.

Spin

The door is open   lid off
the shoebox   I sift through
images   buried ugly snapshots
blood and bone   bare folded
shame   some say better left
in memory's grave.   I stand
before rooms of strangers   and spin
these stories   petals
strewn   blooms bruised
until this magician   pulls out a bouquet
and shaky hands   reach for stems.
You tell me   to stop speaking
in metaphor   but I cannot
peel my skin   and light shimmers
brightest   on the surface   of a black pond.

Wild Women

Some say wild women
are of their own making, wanton
creatures roaming the night
like cats in heat, howling and screeching
once their claws sink
into some poor, unsuspecting mate's back.
I've known them to be more hungry
predators following the scent of fresh meat,
rendered helpless by intoxication—
or granted permission by it.

I've known lost women, more
hunted than hunter, ones
who misplaced cars, clothes, purses—
but most of all their dignity—
(this in pursuit of touch)
after whichever last drink
sent them slinking
into the cave of oblivion,
not by choice, but by compulsion
seeded and growing in their veins.

I've known women
whose eyes first burn
fierce, like an animal caught
in the iron jaws of a trap, then
fade into dullness
as their flame is nearly
doused, drenched
they flail, tethered
by their own desires grown pathetic
and dangerous in alcohol's distortion.

I've known women
who yearn wild
for what will kill them.

Cocoon

By the bottle or by the pill,
fueled for isolation;
brick and mortar added to the wall
growing stronger every day.
Needles spin
webs inside skulls.
Gold and paper
pad the nest
of voices too bright
for our nighttime eyes.
Chrysalis shells
calcify,
reverse metamorphosis,
as desiccated wings
flake-off,
brains wither
and hardened bodies
cocoon.

The Failure of Geographic Cures

I.
In the late '80's, you and your husband
stood before a 10-foot tall
Mickey Mouse, labeled "Ronald Ray-Gun,"
in Amsterdam's Madame Tussauds Wax Museum.
President Mickey packed nuclear missiles
in each pocket. You thought you could live
in a country whose politics molded to your own.

You perused hash listed on a coffee shop menu,
not corned beef and potatoes, but gold or black
with country of origin. Bags of pot earned
their own subheading. This was a country
where you could get away from drinking, dry out
with marijuana. You ordered the blonde
from Lebanon and lit up.

You pedaled your rickety bike to the Bulldog
in Leidseplein, parked beneath the block-headed logo.
The new-country deal was sealed
when you locked onto the green,
almond-eyed Turk. His London accent
offered you a beer. You ditched the husband,
moved to Holland within a year.

II.
John Mayall's brother ran a corner coffee shop
you passed every day enroute to the Centrum.
Besides caffeine, he served booze,
which always goes with the blues.
You hitched your bike outside often;
before you knew it, you were guzzling
beer with the regulars.

You wobbled your drunk bike
rushing to beat green eyes home,
spilled blood on cobbled sidewalks.
There was no hiding
your state when you stumbled-in.
You watched your previously so-cool lover
throw rage at the walls.

You and chaos boarded the plane
bound for Boston, arrived back the night
before signing for your divorce. Sure,
you would miss legal Mary Jane
and *pommes frites* with spicy mayo,
but the old you had caught up.

Otherworld

So many Irish, the most
of any American city, even the one
where descendants dye the river
green in fealty. I noticed
when I lived in Boston
I felt less pink than anyplace else.

I followed ancestors down
cobblestones, ducked into sessions,
tin whistles and fiddles spun tunes
from some deep dwelling within. The drink,
too, striking a chord buried
in ancient Celtic memory.

Gaelic painted gold
overhung doorways, *Roisin Dubh*,
black roses poured into pint glasses,
thick black stout filling empty bellies, drink
drowning famine, a time when hunger
drove more than a million from *Eire*.

I stayed in Boston twenty years,
the same interval as Druidic training.
Twenty years passed as seven, stalled
in the netherworld of pubs and drugs
and youth. I fled something dark,
like my Celtic countrymen, sought a new world

by traveling across the Western Sea;
invited by fairies, we boarded vessels
bound for the Otherworld, transformed
ourselves, defunct druids
and drunks reborn
as scribes, judges,
and poets.

Awakening

> *"This sense of clean and beautiful newness within and without is one of the commonest entries in conversion records...And that such a glorious transformation as this ought of necessity to be preceded by despair ..."*
> —William James in *The Varieties of Religious Experience*

Without ghost lines of turned-down pages,
I pulled the unread book from its wedged perch,
opened to a tale written by a drunk sage.
Without ghost lines, no turned-down pages,
I unlocked the door of my cage—
from weathered story sprung the answer to my search.
Without ghost lines of turned-down pages,
I awakened in this printed church.

For the Irish Girl Who Got Sober (Again) on St. Paddy's Day on a Cruise Ship

Floating cities are inescapable
vessels of temptation

for the lass with a taste
for the drink,

or any substance that muffles
the chatter of voices.

She felt as if the boat
hit an iceberg mid-Caribbean

when he said her bathing suit body
looked too big; she popped a pill,

again lured by the *I'm not good enough* song.
She searched for support to stop the leak.

Buoyed by a meeting flyer
posted on *Shipboard News,*

fellow drunks helped her bail-out
as soon as she started to sink.

That's when she righted herself,
patched the hull enough

to walk past the gauntlet
of midship revelers on St. Paddy's Day—

one man proffered
a cocktail with a tiny green parasol,

opened as if it covered
the mayhem swishing beneath.

*St. Paddy's Day, when amateurs
practice overindulgence.*

She shook her head *no*,
marched past impulse,

skimming the surface
on an ocean of drink.

Two Ships

Adrift, two ships in the night, invisible to one another in the darkness.

My account is low, I need another check/ where is the pre-tax money going?/ I need someone to share my bed/ you snore, I have no desire/ l need you to listen, I need you to care/ this isn't important, there is no pay/ Where is your spirit?/ You pour yourself a drink/ I go to a meeting, to get it back/ Your silence breathes, you explode / I say too much, I sink the ship/ Your vodka has four olives, you float on the surface/ my cup remains empty, I drown within.

In front of the flickering screen, you search/ Behind my words, I am lost. You say I am too fleshy/ I cushion myself against your barbs. Too many hours spent tossed across the waves. Unable to tread water, I slip below the surface / Just stop, you say/ I poison myself, powerless/ I am going out to drink/ I will sing my songs. Where is your spirit? It is buried beneath. My spirit is with me, I am sailing away.

Two ships drift apart at sea.

Dispirited

No more spirits
warming me from the inside,
courage in a jewel-colored bottle
seducing me with elegant charm.
Villain cloaked in convivial company,
you beguiled me with warm laughter
and your rich voice.
I know how you exploited
my dreamy eyes and my wistful heart—
you promised me the mystique of a beautiful woman,
you clothed me in bravado.
You knew I would love you,
that I would wrap my legs around your neck.
The memory of you sometimes sparkles,
scent of warm red oak fills my nose,
your beaded sweat beckons,
tinkling ice in crystal captures
warm amber embraces,
nostalgia for the love affair
of wild abandon dances.
But my spirit now comes
from a deeper well—
my hands grasp cool stone,
I lift fresh, rejuvenating water
to my lips.

Amends to My Father, 1941

In this photo, father stood on a lush front lawn,
a grand Tudor in the distance. His hair was full, leafed-out
like the maples framing him, their limbs wind-tossed,
his hair blown-back from his forehead. This was before
medical school, his brow unlined, clear eyes looking
beyond the lens, not yet hidden behind the glasses
years of study would bring.

This was before he sat beside mother
in theology class, before they chose wedding bands,
before the children started coming, one
after the other, six children in eight years. This was before
he worked twelve-hour stints in the hospital, before
his sick patients devoured him, before his name
was a sweetness melting on his family's tongue.

This was before one daughter ducked behind tombstones
in the cemetery up the street, passed bottles of Boone's Farm
Strawberry Hill, stuffed her bed at night and slithered
down a tree, before she pushed the car in neutral
and sped away, before she blacked-out, before
she almost OD'd on pills, before she crashed
and shattered her boyfriend's vertebrae, before spilled blood
filled her, before three days unconscious, before
nurses propped that broken bird in a chair, before father
had to turn away as her head bobbed down to her chest.

This was before that daughter slapped his Catholic faith,
fled the country, shacked-up in a foreigner's flat,
before she boomeranged back, punched him
again with the sin of divorce.

This was sixty-three years before she broke
from the bottle, before she stretched
across six hundred miles, three times a year,
to clasp his wasted hand while they walked.
This was before Alzheimer's stole
his fine mind, before blank spaces
intruded on their renewed bond—our bond,

Dad, this was seventy-five years before I lost you.

Ghost Bartender

Whiff of red wine, fragrant musty oak,
the Hyde House offers its solitary visitor a drink.
Winter's coming winds stir fallen leaves,
rain-streaked century-old panes rattle.
Mistress of Spirits floats
a ghostly arm, pours burgundy in crystal.
Bartender, please, this will drink me
down into days of wine and roses.
I watched that film snap on its reel—
is there a need to see it to the end?
I am no longer in love with my own tragedy,
I've dispelled this mystique.
The clink of glass fades as if it never was;
I climb up the stairs to sleep.

Cocktail Party

Your words shake hands
with silence, an ice cube melting
into a drink. Once, you drank
fire and it pulled your lips
into a smile, warmed your charms,
cooked your blood, opened your bed.

Now, sparkling water with lime
resigns, your tongue talks small,
you eat too many *hor d'oeuvres*,
and you're a spectator to seduction.
You see laughter get in another car
       and drive away.

Thawing with Frost

I.
We are becoming better acquainted
here in the woods, where I walk
with my own shadowy November guest.
The colors of October have muted brown,
bare branches become their own beauty.
Icicles hang like sharp crystal teeth
from sandstone lips, at once threatening,
then whimsical popsicle in the hand of a young girl.
I hike to Old Man's Cave; a panoramic from inside
looks like an eye open
to the world. Teenagers teargas silence
with echoes of rock
blasting nature's cathedral. I wish
they hadn't come in; I'm sure
they hadn't been invited. But
Eastern Hemlocks stand, unbowed
birches willing to let all of us pass.
Twilight's silver pulls me
out of the gorge, numb fingers
curled-up inside my gloves.

II.
My aged anthology and I
sink without qualms
into the steaming claw foot tub
pedestaled at the B & B
on the National Registry of Historic Places.
Frozen fingers and toes thaw
in the company of Frost, who
may or may not condone my use
of a highlighter on his verse.
I study as I soak, eucalyptus rising.
Afterwards, overheated,
I sneak to the street
and blow smoke into frigid air.

In midnight's pitch, the only soul
who sees, besides me,
is a cat silhouetted in a window
across the way. I know he won't tell
my secret; he's discreet. He's another
acquainted with the night.

Thirteen Ways of Looking at Cowboy Boots

(Hat tipped to Wallace Stevens)

I.
Among the crowd of footwear
standing in her closet,
she chooses the androgynous black cowboy boots.

II.
She was of two minds,
like her stylish yet functional
leather cowboy boots.

III.
Despite their advancing age, the cowboy boots emitted
the musky aroma of a new buck.

IV.
A woman and a pair of shoes
are one.
A woman and her pair of cowboy boots
are at least two.

V.
She doesn't know which she prefers,
the seductress in high-heeled boots,
or the shit-kicking, tough-talking cowgirl
ruling in her cowboy boots,
or both.

VI.
Fine lines etched her mirrored reflection
with unforgiving age.
The polished gleam of the cowboy boots
passed her eye, caught her attention.
She hesitated at the shine of the easily-renewed boots,
an indescribable sadness weighed her down.

VII.
O Cowboys of the Wild West,
could you have imagined over a hundred years hence
a gentlewoman wearing your boots, prancing around, shopping,
dancing, loving in the boots you rode brokeback saddle in?

VIII.
She knows a virile Western twang and the Southern drawl
of a charmer, the rugged outdoorsy cadences of some men;
but she knows, too, the lilting feminine voice of a Northern girl,
and she is definitely wearing cowboy boots.

IX.
When the cowboy boots are put away,
the imprint of their power remains
on her choices.

X.
At the sight of her pulling-on her black or tan cowboy boots,
even the critics of haute couture
applaud her versatile fashion sense.

XI.
She drove all over the Midwest
in a black minivan.
Once, she cried she was lost,
alone in this stampede.
The cut of her boot reminded her
to start walking.

XII.
The river is moving.
Her cowboy boots must be mud-streaked by now.

XIII.
Her whole, tired life was a new frontier.
She was breathing,
and she willed to keep breathing.
Her cowboy boots kicked-up the dust under her feet
as she walked into the sunset.

House of Trees

Morning dew soaks my toes
as I slip into the symphony
of the woods: steady electrical hum
of cicadas, distant crows cawing, soft
twittering birds, luted warbling of thrushes,
the staccato timpani of falling acorns.

Early autumn sun scorches
my skin, until the canopy spreads
a blanket of cool shade
over me. I inhale sweet perfume
of decaying leaves with
earthen undertones.

I've heard the woods
can heal you; trees
emit beneficial compounds
science has isolated. I turn
this over as I look at the rows of trees
standing in loose formation, an army

of vertical guards: elms, tulip poplars,
sugar maples, oaks, all
waiting to envelop me in protective arms.
My footsteps crunch as I approach
a great tree fallen, lying on a soft bed
of layered brown leaves. I cannot

be saddened when I see
how the forest has closed in
on this downed sentinel, draped him
with greenery and orange-spotted jewelweed—
how the dead become
part of the living.

Hymn

We each have our own version of a higher power.
I find mine in the silence of snowflakes
hushing over a city,
or a divine moment like entering fragrant woods
stippled by sunlight.
I, too, crave rain,
when the mist kisses my skin
until I feel bathed like a newborn baby.
I'm a sinner willing
to be baptized again by a new God,
tears couched in raindrops.
Other times, sun's heat penetrates me,
cicadas buzz like electric currents in the air,
energy jolting, or better put, power resurging,
singing a hymn that I am
not a low hum but,
oh, so much more luminous
than I once believed.

Sliver of Power

We sheltered from August steam under fluttering oak leaves,
crescent moon shadows multiplying at our feet.
As moon began to overtake sun, we
stepped beyond shade to stand
where we were scorched
just moments before—
it was as if we stood
the same ground
on a different day,
twenty degrees cooler,
the sun's light filtered
to a temperature more akin
to an autumn afternoon. Light
slipped from summer's buttery yellow
to silvery sheen, the supernatural glow before
violent thunderstorms; birdsong silenced and crickets
soon filled the void with nighttime chirping. We hushed
as moon slid across sun, yet marveled at the power of sun,
who gave so much light with the smallest fraction of herself.

Cameo Moon

This evening a full moon,
cameo white,
hung low in the inky sky,
as if too heavy to rise
above the torches of industry
burning just below.

An inescapable chill
inhabited me today;
scapular muscles contracted
in aching protest, as if
my wings were paralyzed
by the cold.

Weighted,
I sink into the warmth
of minerals suspended.
Am I, too, destined
to remain tethered low,
like the moon?

My icy body thaws
as the bath water cools;
I replenish the heat
in a protracted reverie,
muscles loosening
in the solace of water.

I return to the moon,
now bright white
and risen high in its inevitable arc.
I walk briskly in the blue light,
exhaling puffs of clouds, my body
holding warmth despite the winter air,
again hopeful for the possibility
of ascent.

Resurrection

My hanging baskets are half-dead,
lobelia greens gone brown
with rare white blooms waving.
Forty years after my near-miss
with death's unblooming, fading
life holds me still. I pull dried twigs
and cut-back spent flowers, fertilize
the soil and drench the containers.
Now it's a waiting game
to see if they can recover; I did,

      despite loss of blood
         and consciousness.
              What if

that late-night passerby hadn't found us,
my love crawling on a curve in the road?
My vital signs were flagging
when I was wheeled into Emergency,
a firefly flickering in the dark.
My sister told me I repeated myself
for days after I opened my eyes,
a song stuck in staccato; they worried
my brain had been hit too hard
to be what it once was.

      But I was patched together,
         I healed, I returned
            green and growing.

So, I tend to dying things,
I do not give-up easily.
I turn on the hose and soak
the plants until water runs out.

Additional Acknowledgements

Certain poems were inspired by other fine poems:

A line in "Spin" ("you tell me to stop speaking in metaphor") is from a poem by Erica Manto-Paulson.
"Thirteen Ways of Looking at Cowboy Boots" was inspired by "Thirteen Ways of Looking at a Blackbird," by Wallace Stevens.
"Hymn" was written in response to "Fanlight" by Jeanne Wagner.
Influences from the following Robert Frost poems are woven into "Thawing with Frost": "Birches," "My November Guest," and "Acquainted with the Night."
A line from "When I Think About Cats," by Francesca Bell, inspired "Wild Women."

The poet wishes to thank her writing sisters at Women Writing for a Change, as well as fellow poets in Pauletta Hansel's poetry workshops. Many thanks to family and friends who have lent support along the way, especially Jolly Li and Mary Austin.

Ellen Austin-Li was born and raised in Syracuse, New York. She received her BS in Nursing at Boston College in 1980, then lived and worked in Boston as a pediatric critical care nurse for eighteen years. She moved to Cincinnati, Ohio with her husband, where they started a family. After raising her two sons, Ellen decided to take a class at Women Writing for a Change. There she discovered her passion for words.

Ellen writes poetry and memoir. She has participated in numerous writing workshops in the Cincinnati area, including ongoing poetry workshops facilitated by Pauletta Hansel (Cincinnati's first poet laureate). She has attended several workshops at the University of Iowa Summer Writing Festival. Ellen is an award-winning poet, published in *Artemis, Amethyst Review, Writers Tribe Review, the Maine Review, Mothers Always Write, Memoir Mixtapes, Pine Mountain Sand and Gravel,* and *For a Better World* (2013-2108), among other places.

This is her first collection.